COLLINS AURA GARDEN

CONIFERS

KENNETH A. BECKETT

COLLINS

Products mentioned in this book		
'Clean-Up'	contains	tar acids
'Picket'	contains	permethrin
'Sybol'	contains	pirimiphos-methyl
'Weedol'	contains	diquat/paraquat

Products marked thus '*Sybol*' are trade marks of Imperial Chemical Industries plc
Read the label before you buy: use pesticides safely.

Editor Maggie Daykin
Designers James Marks, Steve Wilson
Picture research Moira McIlroy

This edition first published 1988 by
William Collins Sons & Co Ltd
London · Glasgow · Sydney
Auckland · Toronto · Johannesburg

© Marshall Cavendish Limited 1985, 1988

All rights reserved. No part of this publication may be reproduced or transmitted in any form or by any means, electronic or mechanical, including photocopying, recording or any information storage and retrieval system now known or to be invented without permission in writing from the publisher and copyright holder.

British Library Cataloguing in Publication Data

Beckett, Kenneth A.
    Conifers.——(Collins Aura garden handbooks).
    1. Conifers 2. Ornamental trees
    I. Title
    635.9'7752   SB435

ISBN 0–00–412377–8

Photoset by Bookworm Typesetting
Printed and bound in Hong Kong by Dai Nippon Printing Company

Front cover: Cones of *Cedrus atlantica glauca*
Back cover: Metasequoia glyptostroboides
Both by the Harry Smith Horticultural Photographic Collection

CONTENTS

Introduction	4
Uses in the Garden	9
Pines, Firs, Spruces and their Allies	14
Cedars, Larches and True Cypresses	16
False and Leyland Cypresses and Others	18
Junipers	22
Yews and others	24
Propagation	26
Cultivation	28
Pests and Diseases	30
Sixty of the Best	32

INTRODUCTION

Conifer is not only a name to describe the large areas of afforestation around the British Isles, it also stands for a group of attractive, mainly evergreen trees and shrubs of great value in the garden. Conifers of one sort or another have been grown in gardens for centuries, but never before has there been such a variety to choose from nor such enthusiasm for their planting. And their attraction is not hard to understand when one considers the wide range of shapes, colours, textures and general ease of cultivation, all adding up to year-round appeal.

Garden with conifers

INTRODUCTION

What then are conifers, that they merit a plant category all to themselves, distinct from the general run of trees and shrubs?

It is usual to classify trees and shrubs into two categories: broad-leaved and conifers, though in popular parlance, the "broad-leaved" is often left out, and one then has trees, shrubs and conifers. The broad-leaved category has leaves with a distinct blade, as do most deciduous trees; for example, beech, sycamore, magnolia. They also have recognisable flowers (though sometimes lacking petals), followed by berries or seed pods.

Conifers, in an evolutionary sense, are older and more primitive. Their leaves are generally very small and scale- or needle-like in shape, tough and leathery in texture and often lined or suffused blue-white or grey. They are usually arranged in plumes or fern-like sprays which build up into pyramids, spires or columns of architectural form. Conifers also lack true flowers. Their reproductive organs are called strobili (singular, strobilus) and consist of single-sexed spikes or clusters of tiny, scale-leaves carrying naked ovules or pollen sacs. After the wind-blown pollen has fertilised the ovules, the female strobili become the familiar woody cones, from which comes the name conifer.

Conifers come in almost every shape imaginable: flat mats, hummocks, buns, tables, broad to slender pyramids, spires and columns. Each shape comes in a variety of colours, shades and textures; the permutations are endless. Sizes too vary enormously, from forest trees in excess of 30m (100ft), to mat-formers of 10cm (4in) or less in height.

Marvellous though a group of large cedars, firs or spruces looks in

INTRODUCTION

FAR LEFT A large, well grown specimen of *Chamaecyparis lawsoniana* 'Ellwoodii'.
LEFT A spray of *Pinus sylvestris* (Scots pine) showing male strobili.
BELOW The whipcord-like adult and awl-shaped greyer juvenile foliage of *Juniperus chinensis* is often mixed together. The rounded fruits ripen in the second year. A key ornamental juniper in garden design.

INTRODUCTION

the right setting, few gardens are large enough for them. For this reason it is the smaller species, varieties and cultivars that have come to the fore in recent years. Quite a number of these are so-called "dwarf conifers" and this term can be confusing.

Conifers are very prone to producing mutations (sports). These may occur in the embryo stage within the seed, producing an aberrant seedling, or on a branch of an adult tree. The mutant may differ in foliage details and colour, vigour of growth and ultimate size. True dwarf conifers are mutants that grow slowly and stay small. Others, though sometimes classified as dwarf conifers, are merely slower growing than normal and eventually get big. A good example is the Ellwood cultivar of Lawson's cypress (*Chamaecyparis lawsoniana* 'Ellwoodii'). It starts slowly and stays neat and small for some time, then it gradually builds up vigour and can exceed 5m (15ft); hardly a plant for the rock garden where it is so often planted.

Even the true, very slow-growing dwarf has its "dangers". Being of mutant origin it is prone to mutate back (revert) to its original species form. Some dwarf cultivars are more prone to this than others, especially if they are grafted – as is so often the case – cuttings being difficult or slow to root. Dwarf forms of needle-leaved conifers, such as firs (*Abies*), spruces (*Picea*) and pines (*Pinus*) seem more likely to revert than other conifers. Plants rooted from cuttings are much less likely to do this, but it can happen, so any strong shoot growing from a dwarf should be promptly removed.

Another facet of conifer life that sometimes puzzles the beginner is the occasional startling changes in foliage, shape, size and colour that occur naturally in any one species or cultivar. Many conifers in the seedling and young plant stage have foliage different from that of later on. This is known as juvenile foliage. For example, if a pine is raised from seed – very easily done – the seedling has densely-borne but solitary leaves often much greyer than the adult. After a while, anything from a few months to a few years, the typical bundles of needle leaves arise and gradually take over. Many conifers with scale leaves, such as arbor-vitae (*Thuja*), true cypress (*Cupressus*), false cypress (*Chamaecyparis*) and junipers, have awl-shaped juvenile foliage. Junipers differ from the other examples in that some species stay juvenile all their lives, while others develop adult-type scale leaves.

Some of the mutants that arise perpetuate the juvenile phase or period as it is known. A good example is Fletcher's form of Lawson cypress (*Chamaecyparis lawsoniana* 'Fletcheri'). In the past, these juvenile forms completely fooled botanist and gardener alike, to such an extent that a new genus *Retinospora* was invented to cover them. Under this name have appeared forms of *Chamaecyparis obtusa*, *C.pisifera* and *Thuja occidentalis*; a nice example of plants hoodwinking man, if only for a while.

Juvenile foliage can appear on mature plants. This may occur regularly and naturally in some junipers, notably *Juniperus chinensis* and *J.virginiana*, or as a result of damage. Most pines when cut down never sprout from the stump as broad-leaved trees do, but one of the exceptions is *Pinus canariensis*, the half-hardy Canary Island pine. When cut down, or if branches are removed, shoots occur that are like seedlings in leaf form and colour.

USES IN THE GARDEN

Conifers have two primary roles in the garden, functional and purely ornamental. The roles are not entirely distinct however. Hedges and windbreaks can be pleasing in themselves and make a splendid foil for more colourful plants. Specimen conifers, large or small, can be so grouped to give protection to lesser plants.

Windbreaks or Screens Conifers can make splendid wind barriers. Many of them are native to open hill or mountainsides and so are well adapted to exposed sites, breaking and filtering the wind's force in a natural way. If the right sorts for the site are planted, no pruning should be needed and the normal attractive habit of the individual members of the barrier can be appreciated.

Selecting the right species for the site means having due regard for its ultimate height and spread and the size of the garden to be sheltered. For example, Austrian pine (*Pinus nigra*), makes a splendid windbreak, but ultimately it becomes a large, spreading tree, a row of which would be much too big for any garden of under an acre.

For the smaller garden, it is better to choose a tree with a naturally narrow habit such as Lawson cypress (*Chamaecyparis lawsoniana*) or the ubiquitous but indispensable Leyland cypress (X *Cupressocyparis leylandii*). The latter has speed of growth and density, two prime requisites for a screen. It will also

A stately row of spruces makes a fine background and an efficient windbreak for a large garden such as this one.

USES IN THE GARDEN

ABOVE *Taxus baccata* 'Standishii', a perfect choice for the small garden. The dark green leaves are richly suffused golden yellow.
LEFT A golden Lawson cypress, a green fir and a blue spruce make a splendid specimen trio for a large garden.

stand pruning if necessary and still look pleasing, whereas a fir or spruce will not. Leyland however, should not be used *ad nauseam* if there is an alternative. Western red cedar (*Thuja plicata*) is fast growing and wind firm and some of the hemlocks, such as *Tsuga canadensis* and *T.heterophylla* have distinction.

Hedges Several conifers rank with the best evergreen broad-leaved hedging plants. Whatever is chosen, it must be vigorous and stand up to regular clipping to a restricted shape. Many conifers come into this category, but clipping renders them unsightly. For this reason spruces, firs and pines are to be avoided. Yew (*Taxus baccata*) and the hybrid *T.X media* undoubtedly take pride of place, making the nearest approach to a living wall in density and appearance. Yew is classified as slow-growing, but when established it can put on 15-25cm (6-10in) or more per annum, which is all one can expect from privet after shearing to encourage bushiness. Somewhat faster is *Chamaecyparis lawsoniana*, especially the selected cultivar 'Green Hedger'.

USES IN THE GARDEN

Less common conifers worth trying are the Chinese arborvitae (*Thuja orientalis*) and common juniper (*Juniperus communis*). Leyland cypress is not to be despised, but it is over-planted as a hedge and seems to resent constant hard shearing to 2m (6ft) or less in height. It certainly takes shearing well up to 3m (10ft) or so and makes a pleasing background to a flower border. At the present time, golden Leyland (X *Cupressocyparis leylandii* 'Castlewellan') is popular for hedging. It certainly makes a good hedge, but a concentrated wall of gold can be very over-powering and unsatisfactory as a background to the garden, or as a foil for flowers.

Ground cover The practice of planting low-growing plants of dense habit to cover the ground and prevent weed growth has become very popular in recent years. Plants for this purpose, in addition to their smothering abilities, should be pleasing to look at, if not downright attractive. Among the conifers there are several excellent candidates. Most of the best kinds are junipers (*Juniperus*), a large and varied genus virtually neglected except by enthusiasts until the ground cover movement got underway. Now there are dozens of differing kinds, a surprising number of which are available from nurseries and garden centres. Some have scale leaves, others

A pleasing group of three pygmy pines: the grey-blue *Pinus pumila* 'Globe', the yellow-green *P. mugo* 'Ophir' and the small-leaved *P. mugo* 'Humpy'.

USES IN THE GARDEN

the juvenile-type awl-shaped ones; both come in a wide range of shades of green, grey, purple and blue. The growth may be "spiky" or "fluffy", ground-hugging or with horizontal stems held stiffly just above the soil.

In the fluffy, ground-hugging category, *J.conferta* is probably the best. A native of sandy coasts in Japan and sometimes called Japanese shore juniper, it does well in light, dryish soils in full sun, but is surprisingly adaptable. In the same category are several forms and cultivars of common juniper (*Juniperus communis*) 'Repanda' is one of the best and the greyer 'Hornibrookii' is also good. Really flat are some of the cultivars of *J.horizontalis*, and several of these are justifiably popular, especially the faster growers such as 'Emerald Spreader', 'Bar Harbor' and 'Glauca'. Readily obtainable and often planted purely for ornament or ground cover is the Pfitzer juniper, *J.X media* 'Pfitzerana'). This is not a plant for restricted areas. In time it can become up to 2.4m (8ft) tall and 3m (10ft) or more wide.

Among the non-juniper ground coverers, *Microbiota decussata* is well worth trying. It is much like a prostrate arbor vitae (Thuja) and turns bronze during the winter.

Accent and specimen trees The shapes, colours and textures of many conifers make them pre-eminent as specimens and to grace accent points in the garden. Cedars, particularly the Atlas and Lebanon sorts (*Cedrus atlantica* and *C.libani*) respectively, make noble specimens for a spacious lawn in front of a mansion, but are hopelessly out of place in any garden

Juniperus sabina 'Tamariscifolia' has been cultivated for more than 200 years and is a first rate garden plant.

USES IN THE GARDEN

Chamaecyparis obtusa 'Crippsii' is a delightful, small, slow-growing tree with frond-like golden foliage. It received a First Class Certificate from the Royal Horticultural Society way back in 1899 and still continues in popularity.

under 1 acre and look hideous if cut about to keep them within bounds. For lesser gardens, something slimmer is needed and nothing fits the bill better than the Serbian spruce from Yugoslavia (*Picea omorika*). Even this however, is too big for a plot of less than ⅛ acre. For smaller gardens the slow-growing Korean fir (*Abies koreana*) should be tried, or one of the slim, compact cultivars of *Chamaecyparis lawsoniana*, such as 'Kilmacurragh' or 'Columnaris'. For the tiny garden there is the old gold "miniature" Irish yew, *Taxus baccata* 'Standishii', or that narrowest of all junipers, 'Skyrocket'.

Specimen and accent plants can also be grown in tubs or other containers to grace a patio, terrace or corner. Smaller species and cultivars are needed for this purpose and among the many available the following are worth trying: *Chamaecyparis lawsoniana* 'Ellwoodii', *C.obtusa* 'Crippsii', *C.pisifera* 'Boulevard', *C.p.*'Plumosa Aurea' and *Picea glauca* 'Albertiana Conica'.

Some of the really small dwarf conifers make interesting accent plants for the rock garden or the raised bed. Over-planted, but still the best of its type, is the pigmy Irish juniper *J.communis* 'Compressa', its tight grey columns rarely over 30cm (1ft) tall. Lawson cypress has produced several buns and globes, notable being 'Minima Glauca' and the larger 'Minima Aurea'. Hinoki cypress (*Chamaecyparis obtusa*) from Japan has given rise to equally charming dwarfs of similar size, such as the 60-90cm (2-3ft) 'Nana Gracilis'. It has also yielded the tiniest of mutant conifers, *C.o.*'Minima', perfect for a small sink or bowl garden.

Selected to blend with each other or make pleasing contrasts of habit and colour, conifers can be used most effectively to fill beds and borders. For example, a bed set in grass near the house could be planted with a collection of low junipers in shades of gold, blue, grey and deep green. Farther from the house a smallish specimen tree, say the intense blue-grey *Picea pungens* 'Koster' would look splendid against the winter bronze and summer gold of *Juniperus communis* 'Depressa Aurea'.

In gardens of ½ acre and upwards larger conifers can be grouped to create a major feature. For example, a group of two or three Serbian spruces (*Picea omorika*) flanked by the yellow *Chamaecyparis lawsoniana* 'Stewartii'. More subtle but equally or more satisfying would be a group composed of not less than two oriental spruce (*Picea orientalis*) and one Serbian spruce.

PINES, FIRS, SPRUCES AND THEIR ALLIES

Best described as typical conifers, these are widely planted for forestry and ornament in parks and gardens. They are all modelled on the best known conifer of all, the Norway spruce or Christmas tree (*Picea abies*).

Each tree consists of an erect, spar-like main stem bearing regular whorls of branches that radiate outwards like the spokes of a wheel. Most distinct in this group and indeed of all conifers, are the pines (*Pinus*). The long leaves are truly needle-like, carried in clusters of usually two, three or five. Each cluster is in fact a tiny, peg-like shoot which arises in the axil of a scale leaf. The cones are more woody than those of other conifers and hang or incline downwards, in some species remaining on the tree for several years. The longest and heaviest of all conifer cones are found in this genus.

More than 70 species of pine are recognised and are found around the northern temperate zone from the arctic circle to the equator. Many are important timber trees and several yield resin which in turn produces turpentine and rosin. Several of the smaller sorts are satisfying and attractive plants. Scots pine (*P.sylvestris*) is one of these, particularly the dwarf form 'Beauvronensis' and the winter gold-leaved 'Aurea'. Very decorative also are the slow-growing bristle-cone pine (*P.aristata*), with its white resin dotted leaves, and the smaller forms of *P.leucodermis*. For really tiny pines there are *P.mugo* 'Humpy' and 'Mops'.

Firs (*Abies*) and spruces (*Picea*) are often confused by the novice. Their densely borne, short leaves are usually distinctly flattened and

Although not fully hardy in severe winters, the Mexican *Pinus montezumae hartwegii* is a most decorative pine.

solitary. If erect cones are present, then it is an *Abies;* if the cones are pendulous, it is a *Picea;* but check also the characters of Douglas fir, hemlock and cedar which follow. A surer guide is the way the leaves are carried on the stem. *Picea* stems are grooved and each leaf appears to arise on a tiny, peg-like projection. *Abies* stems are smooth and each leaf has a rounded, sucker-like base which pulls away cleanly when mature. However, there is one conifer that resembles a picea in foliage but is not. This is the Douglas fir (*Pseudotsuga menziesii*). If the tree is mature enough to bear cones, these alone easily distinguish it. Each pendent cone has hooded scales from which project very conspicuous, tongue-like bracts.

LEFT *Tsuga canadensis* 'Jeddeloh' is one of the most promising newer cultivars of the Canadian hemlock.
BELOW *Picea pungens* 'Glauca Moerheimii' is a good form of the blue spruce for medium-sized gardens.

The hemlock spruces (*Tsuga*) are distinct from the above in their very slender stems, wispy tops, somewhat yew-like leaves of varying sizes and mainly very small cones – less than 2.5cm (1in) long in the commonest species.

Comparatively few firs and spruces are small enough for the average garden. *Abies koreana* is good and has already been mentioned. *A.delavayi* one of the silver firs, is larger but even more handsome. One of the best and most useful of the dwarfs is *A.balsamea* 'Hudsonia', a perfect shrub for the rock garden.

Of the spruces, *Picea omorika* has already been mentioned, also *P.pungens* and its blue forms. *P.brewerana* is the most elegant of all the spruces; however, it slowly but surely gets big. Among the several dwarfs are *P.abies* 'Gregoryana', a cushion of 15-20cm (6-8in) and the larger, flat-topped 'Nidiformis'. There is also a tiny form of Serbian spruce, namely, *P.omorika* 'Minimax'.

Douglas fir, *Pseudotsuga menziesii*, is rather large, though it, and its grey-leaved variety *P.m.glauca*, make fine specimen trees for the large garden. There is a dwarf called 'Fretsii' but it is not easy to obtain.

The hemlock spruces also grow large and make elegant specimens but there are several dwarfs also. *Tsuga canadensis* 'Bennett' is attractively semi-prostrate and not much above 30cm (1ft) tall.

Chile pine (*Araucaria araucana*), better known as monkey puzzle, is only a pine by name and surely the one conifer that everyone can recognise on sight. It looks splendid in groups, or as an avenue where there is plenty of room but is quite out of place in a small garden.

CEDARS, LARCHES AND TRUE CYPRESSES

True cedars (*Cedrus*) have characters in common with the spruces and firs but are easily distinguished. Spire-like in habit when young, as they age the upper branches spread and thicken, creating the flat-topped tree familiar on the lawn of past and present mansions. Their needle-like leaves are borne in two ways: vigorously growing stem tips are clad in spirally arranged, fairly well spaced leaves, but mostly they are carried in dense whorls on the tips of very short side branches known as spurs. The barrel-shaped cones stand erect on the branches, breaking up when they are ripe, while still attached to the tree.

Unfortunately, the handsome cones of *Cedrus atlantica* 'Glauca' fall apart when the seeds are fully ripe.

Cedars are handsome trees and specially decorative when young, hence their popularity. In time they get big and can present problems. Pruning totally destroys their natural habit, so they are not recommended for gardens under ½ an acre in extent. Where there is room the deodar (*C.deodara*) is perhaps the most satisfying, being fast growing and remaining an elegant pyramid for longer than the other species. The grey-blue foliage of the blue Atlas cedar (*C.atlantica* 'Glauca') has great appeal and is much planted. For the smaller garden there is *C.a.*'Fastigiata', of erect columnar growth, and the weeping 'Pendula', as broad as it is tall at 10m (30ft).

Larch (*Larix*) has the same foliage formation and a similar growth habit, but deciduous leaves. Also, the cones are small and stay on the tree for two years or more. Larches also get big in time, but are especially decorative when young. Their lovely pale green young foliage alone makes them worthy garden plants. They can be bought fairly cheaply and grow quickly, so there is much to be said for treating them as short term garden decoration. As soon as they get to 3-5m (10-15ft) or as tall as required, they can be cut down and replaced with another. The best species for this treatment is *L.decidua*, the common larch. Its hybrid Dunkeld larch, *L.X eurolepis* is almost as good, but the leaves have blue-grey shading and lack the brilliantly fresh green of *L.decidua*.

Incense cedar (*Calocedrus decurrens* or *Libocedrus decurrens*), is a cedar in name only. It is in fact, closely related to arbor vitae and has similar flattened foliage sprays but with longer scale leaves. The small narrow cones have only three fully-formed scales and the seeds have a long membranous wing at the upper end. Incense cedar is columnar but can grow 60cm (2ft) per annum in moist soils, so it soon becomes a very large tree.

Japanese cedar (*Cryptomeria japonica*) is also a cedar by name only, being more closely allied to the redwoods (*Sequoia*). Its leaves are very distinct, awl-shaped but flattened vertically and with a winged base, the tips tending to curve in towards the stem. Juvenile leaves are longer, softer and spreading, and in the juvenile cultivar *C.j.*'Elegans', they turn reddish bronze in winter. 'Elegans' is of lesser stature and therefore suitable for the smaller garden. For the rock garden, the dwarf, globe-shaped *C.j.*'Vilmoriniana' can be recommended.

True cypresses (*Cupressus*) are distinguished by scale leaves, overlapping along the stems to form a whipcord pattern. The stems branch freely to form three-dimensional sprays. The rounded to ovoid cones are composed of angular, mushroom-shaped scales, each with several seeds. (Some junipers have similar foliage but the cones are berry-like). Only three species and their cultivars are generally cultivated, of which *C.arizonica*, the Arizona cypress with grey foliage and flaking bark, is most garden-worthy *C.a*'Pyramidalis' (*C.glabra* 'Pyramidalis') is more compact and has smooth bark. Monterey cypress (*C.macrocarpa*) is much used as a windbreak near the sea and will stand clipping to form a large, short-term hedge. There are also several not particularly attractive dwarfs, e.g. 'Globosa' and 'Minima' ('Minimax'). The Mediterranean or funeral cypress, *C.sempervirens* forms narrow, dark green, picturesque spires, but it gets big and is not fully hardy.

LEFT *Cedrus deodara*, the deodar, is the most elegant of the true cedars, particularly when young.

ABOVE The grey foliage of the Arizona cypress, *Cypressus arizonica*. It makes a fine specimen for the medium-sized garden.

FALSE AND LEYLAND CYPRESSES AND OTHERS

False cypresses (*Chamaecyparis*) are easily distinguished from the true cypresses by their foliage and cones. The leaves are scale-like but they and the stems are flattened and have an almost two-dimensional appearance. The branches also are frond-like and flattened, whereas those of the true cypress are rounded in cross section.

All the cultivated *Chamaecyparis* are of the narrow pyramid or columnar form and some can become tall in time. However, they have great variety of foliage colour and there are numerous smaller cultivars to choose from. As a result, they are among the most planted of all hardy conifers. Most popular is Lawson cypress *C.lawsoniana*, from N.W. California and S.W.Oregon. Considering its homeland, it is remarkably tough and hardy. The rich green foliage has a curiously pungent aroma and the freely-borne, tiny male strobili are crimson. The normal habit is broadly columnar but there are several variations, from narrow to broad, conical and bun-shaped. A number of cultivars are mentioned elsewhere in this book.

Hinoki cypress, *C.obtusa*, has provided some of the most appealing slow growing and really dwarf cultivars. Among those well worth growing are *C.o.*'Nana Gracilis' with shell-shaped, dark green foliage sprays on bushes to 90cm (3ft); *C.o.*'Graciosa', lacily elegant to 120cm (4ft) or more, and the smaller, yellow-gold 'Nana Lutea'.

Sawara cypress (*C.pisifera*) is seldom grown in its original form but some of its cultivars are understandably popular. Best known nowadays is the juvenile 'Boulevard', fairly slow-growing, shapely and nicely silvered. 'Plumosa Aurea', which is

BELOW LEFT Raised in Holland in 1895, *Chamaecyparis lawsoniana* 'Triomphe de Boskoop' forms a vigorous, broad column and makes a good specimen tree.

BELOW *Chamaecyparis obtusa* 'Nana Gracilis' has been grown for over 100 years and remains one of the best dwarf conifers.

FAR BELOW *Chamaecyparis pisifera* 'Plumosa Aurea Compacta' provides tints of gold and bronze-gold in the heather garden.

semi-juvenile and has yellow young leaves, can attain a good size in time, whereas 'Plumosa Aurea Compacta' ('Plumosa Aurea Nana') stays small and is useful for the rock garden. Commonly planted in the past, and still seen in parks and gardens, is the plumy, grey juvenile, *C.p.*'Squarrosa', which can reach 10m (30ft) or more, but is well worth a place in the larger garden.

Like the sawara cypress, white cypress *C.thyoides*, is virtually never grown in its original tree form, but via mutation it has given us one of the best known of all dwarf cultivars, *C.t.*'Ericoides'. This has sea-green juvenile leaves that take on shades of purple in winter. It is not strictly dwarf, growing 5-7.5cm (2-3in) a year; pyramidal when young, columnar later.

Unlike the previous two species, Nootka cypress, *C.nootkatensis* is invariably grown in its original wild tree state; few cultivars are known and even fewer are readily obtainable. In overall appearance it resembles Lawson cypress but is easily distinguished once it is ten years old or so, by its elegant, pendent branchlets. The cones too are very large for a false cypress and each scale has a pointed boss.

Leyland cypress, X *Cupressocyparis leylandii*, nicely bridges the gap between true and false cypresses, having arisen as a spontaneous hybrid between Nootka and Monterey cypresses at Leighton Hall, Welshpool, Wales, late last century. Its garden values have been touched upon already, its phenomenal speed of growth has not: 31m (100ft) in 50 years is recorded.

Coast redwood, *Sequoia sempervirens*, and the Sierra redwood, *Sequoiadendron giganteum*, are the two largest conifers known. Coast redwood is tallest, at least one

FALSE AND LEYLAND CYPRESSES

specimen of 112.4m (368ft) has been recorded, and that some years ago. They are trees for the largest garden only, though very decorative when young and worth consideration in the short term as for larch (see page 16).

Dawn redwood, *Metasequoia glyptostroboides*, and swamp cypress *Taxodium distichum* are allied and similar deciduous conifers related to the redwoods. They make splendid specimen trees where the soil stays reasonably moist. Dawn redwood is also of considerable interest, being described originally from fossil remains, then discovered growing in China in 1941.

Arbor-vitae, Hiba and Maidenhair According to some authorities, arbor-vitae is the Latinised version of the French *L'arbre de vie* (tree of life), a name reputedly bestowed on *Thuja orientalis* by a king of France in the 16th century.

In overall appearance, the various species of *Thuja* much resemble the false cypresses. However, as soon as cones are present – and these are borne on quite young plants – the two are easily distinguished. Arbor-vitae cones are elongated, composed of at least three pairs of scales with recurved, pointed tips. The most distinctive of all the thujas is the original Chinese species, *T.orientalis*. Usually of large shrub size, it can be columnar or conical to oval in outline. Old specimens often become gaunt, shapeless and very unlike conifers in appearance. The usually freely produced cones with their rolled back scale tips are quaintly decorative. So different is this arbor-vitae that some botanists classify it on its own as *Biota orientalis*. It has given rise to several first rate dwarfs, notably 'Aurea Nana', a 30-60cm (1-2ft) oval gold bush, and the

ABOVE *Chamaecyparis lawsoniana* 'Intertexta' has the most distinctive habit of all the many Lawson cypress cultivars.
RIGHT A swamp cypress, *Taxodium distichum*, in its coppery autumn dress.

larger 'Conspicua' of similar colour.

Western red cedar is a familiar name to owners of greenhouses and to timber merchants, but few people realise it comes from the western arbor-vitae, *Thuja plicata*, yet another cedar by name only. This giant from NW.N.America is too big as a specimen for all but large gardens but it is adaptable and stands clipping well. The most decorative large cultivar is *T.p.*'Atrovirens' with broad sprays of rich glossy leaves; *T.p.*'Zebrina' is also big, but has bands of yellow across the foliage sprays. The newer, more evenly suffused golden-yellow cultivar 'Irish Gold' is slower growing and suitable for the smaller garden. Among dwarfs is the 60 year old

deserve to be recognised: 'Danica' is a globular bush 30-45cm (1-1½ft), dark green in summer, bronze in winter; 'Europe Gold' is narrowly pyramidal to 1.8m (6ft) or more with yellow foliage all the year, while 'Recurva Nana', has bright green, curiously congested foliage which flushes bronze in winter. It grows slowly to about 30cm (1ft) but spreads more widely.

Hiba (the Japanese name) or false arbor-vitae, *Thujopsis dolabrata*, is a tree to 15m (50ft) or more in the wild, but in cultivation it is often seen as a large, dense shrub especially in the eastern half of the country. Tree-sized specimens exist in larger gardens down the west coast from Argyll to Cornwall. Pyramidal to columnar in outline, hiba has much larger, broader, boat-shaped scale leaves that are lustrous, green above and blue-white beneath. *T.d.*'Aurea' foliage is lightly suffused with pale gold. Not commonly seen, it is well worth seeking as a smallish specimen tree. The most commonly seen cultivar is 'Variegata', which usually stays bushy when young and is strikingly splashed with white – though the effect is rather as if dive-bombed by a party of delinquent sparrows.

Maidenhair tree, *Ginkgo biloba* is in no way related to the above, but is fitted in here for convenience. It was once considered to be related to the yew family, but nowadays botanists place it in an order of its own. Technically therefore it is not even a conifer, but so long considered to be one that it must be included. Ginkgo is a deciduous tree with intriguing fan-shaped leaves that turn bright yellow in autumn. Although eventually big it is often very slender when young, will stand quite hard pruning and makes a magnificent specimen tree for the large garden.

'Rogersii', very slow growing to about 45cm (1½ft) or so, and forming a bush of gold. The larger 'Stoneham Gold' is dark green, tipped yellow.

Eastern arbor-vitae, *T.occidentalis* comes from eastern Canada and the U.S.A. and is sometimes confusingly called northern white cedar. Although it thrives well in wet soils, it is seldom cultivated in its original tree form. It has nevertheless managed to produce many dwarf and slow growing mutants of decided garden worthiness. Best known and much planted is 'Rheingold', but there are others that

JUNIPERS

Although obviously conifers in appearance, junipers produce what look like berries. Anatomically, they are real cones but the small scales of which they are formed are fused and fleshy. In general, the leaves are awl-shaped – half-way between a scale and a needle – and are arranged in pairs or whorls. However, some species and varieties have scale leaves only, others have both mixed together.

For the modern garden no other genus of conifers is more useful than *Juniperus*. At least 60 species have been described and many more cultivars are known. Indeed, hardly a year goes by without another new one joining the ranks. Among these can be found every kind of habit and colour: slender spires, pyramids, rounded and flat-topped bushes, hummocks and carpeters in a wide range of greens, blues, greys and yellows.

Junipers are first rate ground cover plants and some of the most reliable and attractive have already been mentioned. There are many more; for example, the strong growing, grey-green *J.sabina* 'Blue Danube'. Intense silvery blue foliage is provided by the aptly named *J.squamata* 'Blue Carpet', a vigorous carpeter to 1.5m (5ft) or more. Pure rich green is less common among the prostrate junipers, so the arrival of *J.communis* 'Green Carpet' is welcome. Dense and not too fast growing, it has deep green leaves except in the summer months when the new growth glows brightly. It was discovered on the rocky coastline near Stavanger in Norway, so is totally hardy.

Where small areas of ground cover are required and neater, slower growing plants can be used, *J.squamata* 'Blue Star' is a must. Steely grey-blue and very compact, it steadily spreads to 60cm (2ft) and rarely tops 30cm (1ft). It combines beautifully with the deep green of *Picea abies* 'Nidiformis' and the golden yellow of *Chamaecyparis lawsoniana* 'Aurea Densa'.

Attractive bushy species and cultivars suitable for beds and borders abound. Bright deep green is provided by *J.chinensis* 'Kaizuka', a semi-erect sort to 180cm (6ft) and more, with scale leaves and foliage sprays like those of a cypress. Though often listed under *J.virginiana*, 'Grey Owl' is now considered to be a hybrid with 'Pfitzerana' (q.v.). It has a similar habit but is

Introduced from Japan about 1920, *Juniperus chinensis* 'Kaizuka' makes a specimen of character for the smaller lawn.

Although already commonly planted, it is worth recording here that *Juniperus* 'Pfitzerana' makes a fine specimen plant for the medium-sized garden. It is also an invaluable conifer for use as ground cover and does not object to shade.

smaller and generally lower. Useful as large ground cover, its smoky-grey foliage also looks good among other shrubs or on its own at the side of a lawn. If a smaller, denser growing version is required, ultimately to around 150cm (5ft) spread, then 'Blue Cloud' is the one to go for.

J.X media (*chinensis* X *sabina*) contains several coloured and variegated foliage shrubs. Of these, 'Old Gold' is probably the best yellow. It can reach 120cm (4ft) or so and rather more across. 'Silver Spray' has similar dimensions, but looks very different with its sprays of sulphur-white foliage all year.

Among columnar and tree-sized junipers suitable as lawn specimens or other accent points, the alligator or chequer bark juniper, *J.pachyphlaea* (*J.deppeana pachyphlaea*) takes some beating. Columnar in form, ultimately to 10m (30ft) or so, it has the most intense blue-white foliage of any conifer and a well grown specimen automatically becomes a talking as well as an accent point. However, it does need a really well drained soil and a sunny site. Also specimens of quality are *J.recurva* and *J.rigida*. Pyramidal in outline for many years, both have gracefully pendent branchlets clad in fairly long awl-shaped leaves. The best variety is *J.recurva coxii*, which has longer, more pendulous stems and sage-green leaves. For grace however, *J.rigida* just has the edge and its leaves change to bronze in winter.

Tallest of the hardy junipers is *J.virginiana*, confusingly known in its native land as pencil, red and Virginia cedar. In the wild it has achieved 35m (100ft) but there are few above half this height in the British Isles. It is narrowly conical for the first half of its life, when it is very attractive. For the smaller garden *J.v.*'Burkii', densely columnar and bronze-purple in winter, should be sought after, or the attractive, bright green, conical 'Canaertii'.

YEWS AND OTHERS

The group described here contains the least conifer-like, hardy members of their family. Best known are the yews (Taxus), clearly recognised by their curious fruits – sticky, fleshy cups each with one hard seed at the bottom. They look as far removed from a cone as can be but the basic anatomy is right. Female strobili consist of a few scales and a solitary ovule. After fertilisation, the ovule becomes a seed and an extra layer of tissue around its base (arillus) develops into the cup. The scales stay small and soft and can be seen at the base of the yew "berry". Yew leaves are small, narrow and parallel sided, not unlike those of some fir trees.

LEFT Golden Irish yew, *Taxus baccata* 'Fastigiata Aurea' makes an imposing specimen for the larger lawn.

ABOVE The curious, cup-shaped, sticky "berries" of common yew, *Taxus baccata*. One of our few native conifers.

About eight species are known but only two of these and their hybrid is widely grown. By far the largest number of cultivars are derived from the common yew, *Taxus baccata* which is native to Europe, including the British Isles, S.W.Asia and N.Africa. Apart from its use as a first rate hedging plant, common yew is too large and sombre for most gardens.

Irish yew, *T.b.*'Fastigiata' is also large but its broadly columnar habit makes it an acceptable accent point in the larger garden. Better still is 'Fastigiata Aureomarginata', the golden Irish yew with yellow-margined leaves. Wide-spreading but not too tall is *T.b.*'Adpressa' and its gold margined leaved 'Adpressa Variegata'. Both have very short broad leaves that are decidedly un-yew like. Also wide-spreading, but with normal leaves is 'Dovastoniana'. This has tiers of almost horizontal branches clad with pendent branchlets – quite the most elegant of yews. 'Dovastoniana Aurea' is yellow variegated. If a ground-covering yew is needed, 'Repandens' nicely fills the bill, spreading to 1.5m (5ft) but rarely topping 45cm (1½ft) in height.

Yews suitable for the rock garden are few and far between. T.b.'Amersfoort' is more interesting than beautiful, being a small, very slow growing bushlet with well spaced branches and very short thick leaves. Japanese yew, T.cuspidata provides more bushy fare in the form of 'Densa', mound-forming; and 'Minima', a rather picturesquely irregular and very slow growing moppet.

Plum-fruited yew (Cephalotaxus) has larger, enclosed fruits, the fleshy part formed from the outer tissue of the seed. It has similar, but much larger leaves than yew, especially in the Chinese plum yew, C.fortunei. Also known as cow's-tail pine, this is the most handsome of the hardier species, with glossy, deep green sickle-shaped leaves 5-9cm (2-3½in) long. It makes a large shrub in time and can be used as an effective specimen. It has a low growing mutant C.f.'Prostrata' that spreads sideways and makes good ground cover. Hardier is C.harringtonia (C.drupacea on some lists) but it has smaller, paler foliage. Nevertheless it is a worthwhile shrub.

Some members of the genus Podocarpus have fruits like those of Cephalotaxus, others bear fruits like yew berries turned inside out. These latter are formed when the small scales at the base of the seed fuse together and become fleshy. Hardiest in this category and a perfect shrub for the larger rock garden is P.nivalis from the mountains of New Zealand. Regrettably, male and female strobili are carried on separate plants and both are needed for the red fruits to develop.

Unrelated to the above but having leaves remarkably similar to those of the Chinese plum yew is the Chinese fir, *Cunninghamia lanceolata*. Sadly, this handsome species can be damaged in severe winters though it usually recovers. It makes a fine specimen for a sheltered site, eventually forming a columnar tree to 10m (30ft) or more. Smallish, rounded, woody cones are produced, each with toothed, long-pointed scales.

Even without its red fruits, *Podocarpus nivalis* from New Zealand is still worth a place in the garden. The olive green foliage is densely borne and attractive in its own right. If you garden on chalky soil, this is the one for you.

PROPAGATION

While there is a lot of satisfaction to be gained from propagating one's own conifers, it must be realised that in the majority of cases the process takes time. From when the seeds are sown or cuttings taken, it is usually three years before a plant big enough to merit a second glance develops. There are of course exceptions; some pines, true cypresses, Leyland cypress, dawn redwood and others, can be 120cm (4ft) tall or more in that time. A lot depends on climate, soil and situation.

With very few exceptions, all the conifer species are best raised from seed. Cultivars on the other hand rarely come true to type from seed and must be increased by cuttings or grafting. If a few plants only are required, cuttings provide an easy means for most conifers. There are some groups however, which do not root easily, or take a long time to produce shapely specimens: pines, firs and spruces are prime examples.

Some dwarf cultivars, in particular pines, are almost impossible to root. These difficult sorts the nurseryman grafts, this being the only way to produce saleable specimens in a reasonable time if the price is not to be prohibitive. Unfortunately, grafted plants sometimes grow faster and larger than they otherwise would and are more prone to produce reversion shoots.

Cuttings The time honoured nurseryman's way of taking conifer cuttings is in a shady cold frame in autumn, October being the best month. The frame must be screened from direct sunshine, and the foot of a north wall or fence is an ideal location. A mixture of half coarse sand and half medium to fine grade perlite or peat is the best rooting medium, placed in the bottom of a frame 10-15cm (4-6in) deep. Alternatively, pots and boxes can be filled with the mixture and plunged in the soil or preferably sand base of the frame. This is important because during cold spells in winter pots and pans on the surface of the soil, even in a frame, can freeze solid.

The best cuttings are sturdy side shoots formed the previous summer. These are carefully pulled off by grasping the base with thumb and forefinger and levering backwards. The shoot comes away with a sliver or heel of the parent stem and is known as a heel cutting. The tail of the heel is trimmed and the top shortened if necessary so that the overall length does not exceed 10-13cm (4-5in). Any foliage is severed from the basal half of each cutting, the heel base is dipped in 'Keriroot' hormone rooting powder and the cutting is then inserted immediately 4-5cm (1½-2in) apart each way with the lower one third to one half below the surface. One good watering is given and the frame light (top) shut. If the weather stays warm the cuttings should be lightly sprayed over with water daily.

Once November arrives the cuttings can be virtually forgotten until the following February or March. But from April onwards, ventilation and spraying over must be carried out regularly. By the end of May all the easy sorts will be rooted. Any that are not should be left until early autumn. For small quantities the rooted cuttings are best placed singly in 7.5cm (3in) or smaller pots of a standard potting compost. The

1. A *Cryptomeria* branchlet, showing a number of healthy lateral shoots suitable for use as cuttings.

2. Carefully pull away the selected shoot or shoots, so that each has a heel of the parent stem attached.

3. Trim the "tail" of woody tissue away from the heel, then dip the heel in a hormone rooting powder.

4. Insert the cuttings in rows in sandy soil in a cold frame, so about half the stem length is buried.

5. When well rooted, dig up cutting with a hand fork, taking care not to damage the roots, and pot them on separately.

6. Using standard or all-peat potting mix, set each cutting singly in 7.5-10cm (3-5in) container. Place in cold frame.

following autumn or spring, pot-on the young plants into larger containers or plant them out in rows.

Seeds Conifer seeds are best sown in spring in a cold frame, using pots or boxes of a soil-less compost such as 'Kericompost', or direct in a sandy soil in the bottom. Seed must be sown thinly on the surface then covered with about 1cm (2/5 in) of grit and watered. When the seedlings are large enough to handle, prick off in rows in a cold frame or a sheltered bed outside. Or they can be potted singly as for cuttings.

When growing on your cuttings in a nursery bed, keep weeds well at bay.

CULTIVATION

Happily, conifers will grow in the most ordinary of soils provided there is adequate moisture and light. Rich soil is certainly not required; indeed, a soil over-laced with artificial fertilisers is invariably detrimental to growth. A few conifers do have particular preferences. For example, most firs (Abies) need a lime-free soil. Dawn redwood and swamp cypress must have adequate moisture if they are to grow vigorously. The young foliage of some spruces and most firs is susceptible to spring frost damage, so a site not prone to this hazard should be chosen.

Unless one is lucky enough to have a new garden on former, well maintained arable farmland or a small holding, some preparation of the soil will be needed. A first consideration is to eradicate perennial weeds. Use one of the modern herbicides such as 'Weedol' to clean up the site well beforehand. Unless lots of small plants or a hedge are to be planted it is not necessary to dig over the whole site. If overall cultivating is contemplated, single digging is adequate, working in 'Forest Bark' Ground and Composted, or manure.

A new garden may have been partially or totally stripped of its top soil, or contain builders' rubbish, or both. The site should then be roughly forked over, the rubbish removed and more top soil brought in. Subsoil can be made into a fertile growing medium, but it needs lots of bulky humus, such as 'Forest Bark' Ground and Composted, manure, spent mushroom compost or peat worked into it and spread upon the surface. A load of top soil is usually cheaper.

If the site is poorly drained it is seldom worth the expense of tile drains and a soakaway. Better to build raised beds or choose conifers that tolerate such conditions.

Planting Autumn and spring are the best times for planting, though containerised specimens can be put out any time the soil and weather are suitable. In winter, mild weather is best when the soil is not too wet. Dig each hole larger than the root ball of the plant. Add a couple of

1. Dig a hole somewhat larger than the root ball. Add a handful of a fertilizer such as Growmore.

2. Place the plant in the hole so that the top of root ball is about 4cm (1½in) below the surface of the soil.

3. Fill in with soil and firm well in, leaving a shallow depression around the plant for efficient watering.

handfuls of a fertilizer such as Growmore. Set containerised specimens so that when filled in, the top of the root ball is covered with about 2.5cm (1in) of soil. Plants direct from the nursery ground should be placed slightly deeper than they were. Fill in around the roots with a mixture of soil and 'Forest Bark' Ground and Composted, then firm with the fists or feet, depending on the size of the plant. Leave a shallow depression around the plant for watering, especially on light, free-draining soils.

If the site is in a lawn, mark out the planting hole, skim off the turf and place it to one side. Dig the hole, then place the turf in the bottom, root side uppermost. Roughly chop up the turf then cover with enough soil to make it the right depth for planting. It is important to maintain an area of bare soil around lawn specimens for a few years, or until they start growing vigorously because thick grass or weeds will intercept some of the essential water and plant food that the young conifer needs in order to flourish.

Maintenance After planting, the most important aspect of maintenance during the ensuing growing season or two is watering. Unless the soil is of a water retentive nature start watering after two or three weeks without rain. Fill up the depression three times then leave it a week, water again, and so on. Once the roots are down and the plant is growing well, usually two or three years, sometimes less, watering should not be needed. During this period, an annual mulch of 'Forest Bark' Ground and Composted mixed with bonemeal is beneficial. Staking should never be needed for a well grown conifer, but close grown nursery stock of Leyland cypress are often sold with canes. Aim to remove

First recorded in 1829, *Abies balsamea* 'Hudsonia' has long been an indispensable dwarf fir for the rock garden.

these supports as soon as you possibly can.

Pruning Unlike many other trees and shrubs, conifers attain their decorative shapes without initial training and subsequent pruning. However, now and then strong winds or snow will pull a branchlet out of place. This will need tying in or cutting off, whichever best preserves the outline. More rarely, the leading stem of a pine, fir or spruce gets damaged and two or more leaders develop. To preserve the symmetry of the tree the strongest leader must be selected and the others removed. If this sort of damage is observed early on, it is best to tie the strongest of the uppermost horizontal branches vertically to a cane. This usually ensures that only one replacement leader develops.

Hedges of conifers generally need one annual trimming in late summer, though fast growing sorts such as Leyland cypress are best clipped at least twice between mid-summer and early autumn.

PESTS AND DISEASES

Conifers are remarkably free of the common pests and diseases but they do have a few all of their own that occasionally cause problems. When using the insecticides and fungicides recommended, follow exactly the makers' instructions. An under-dose will leave the plant unscathed, an over-dose may not only kill the pest or disease but scorch or otherwise damage the plant.

The following list outlines symptoms easily observable and suggests methods of control.

Leaves browning, particularly of Lawson and other false cypresses. See Whole plant: poor growth.

Leaves with white waxy tufts, see next entry.

Leaves yellow flecked or mottled Leaves of firs, spruces and pines with white waxy tufts and a yellow mottle are suffering from one of the various kinds of adelgids. These are related to aphids (greenfly) but are covered with fluffy tufts of waxy white wool, and suck sap, causing premature leaf fall. The tree is weakened and stems may die back. Spray thoroughly with 'Sybol' as soon as symptoms are observed and repeat at weekly intervals for 4-6 weeks. Spruces, particularly Sitka and blue, may have small greenfly – the green spruce aphid – which causes similar symptoms and responds to a treatment with 'Sybol' spray. See also Whole plant: poor growth.

Leaves rapidly yellowing Complete yellowing, then browning of foliage followed by leaf fall, particularly on dwarf conifers, denotes an attack by conifer spinning mite. A close look will reveal fine threads. The mite is related to the common greenhouse red-spider mite, sucks sap and severely weakens plant tissue. Spray thoroughly with 'Sybol' at the first signs of attack and repeat the process at 7-10 day intervals, until problem clears. See also Whole plant: poor growth.

Needle cast disease on pine is the result of a variety of causes, from root damage to the attack of leaf fungi. If serious, it is worth while spraying with Bordeaux mixture as soon as you spot the problem.

Leaves eaten Various species of pine may be attacked by the larvae (caterpillars) of sawflies and moths. These are green or green and white striped and not easy to see. Spray with 'Sybol' or 'Picket' as soon as damage is observed.

Twigs distorted or with galls Galls resembling miniature pineapples on spruce shoots are caused by the spruce gall adelgid. It sucks sap which results in weakened, poorly-shaped trees. Spray several times in winter with 'Sybol' from November to April, choosing a spell of mild weather. See also Leaves with white waxy tufts.

Twigs and branchlets dying back See Leaves yellow flecked or mottled, Leaves rapidly yellowing and Twigs distorted.

Main stems stripped of bark Young conifers can have all the lower bark and cambium tissue stripped from the stems by rabbits, squirrels, voles or field mice, particularly during hard winters. If the tree is completely ringed it can die. Protecting the stems with special tree guards or rolls of fine mesh chicken wire is effective, but trapping and shooting should be carried out at the same time.

Whole plant: poor growth Small, yellowish or brown sparse foliage, thin short annual growth and partial dieback may be a long term effect of adelgids (See Leaves flecked and Leaves rapidly yellowing) but is more likely to be due to the death of some or all roots, caused by the fungus known as phytophthora root death which attacks a wide range of trees and shrubs.

Among conifers, Lawson cypress and yews are prone to infection.

An extra large specimen of adelgid gall; usually they are more compact.

Apart from the poor growth above, there are symptoms at the base: strips of dead bark may extend up the trunk from the ground and root bases showing at ground level may be dead. Total death of the tree is usually inevitable. At the present there is no chemical cure available to amateur growers. Avoid all kinds of water-logging to prevent the spread of actively swimming spores. Do not transplant infected specimens into clean soil. Avoid nursery stock with brown foliage tips; they may be infected.

Whole plant: sudden death The fairly rapid death of any tree or shrub may be due to honey fungus, which causes withering and ultimate falling or browning of foliage. When the tree or shrub is dug up there may be a sheet of whitish fungal tissue at the base of the stem, just below and at ground level. Among the dead roots will be seen blackish bootlace-like strands, suggesting its alternative name of bootlace fungus. There is no absolute cure but drenching the infected areas with Bray's Emulsion can kill existing disease and protect healthy plants from infection. Do not replant into treated soil for eight months.

SIXTY OF THE BEST

The lists of plants that follow are arranged according to their use in the garden. All are commercially available, though some may have to be searched for. The asterisk denotes a tolerance or love of wet sites.

Evergreen conifers planting

MINIATURES

Chamaecyparis lawsoniana 'Minima Aurea'. First described in 1929, this cultivar forms a densely growing conical bush. The tight sprays of foliage are inclined to twist sideways much in the same way as *Thuja orientalis* and are bright golden yellow all year. It grows about 4cm (1½in) per year, slowing down when older.

Juniperus communis 'Compressa'
Juniperus chinensis 'Echiniformis'

Chamaecyparis lawsoniana 'Minima aurea'

Juniperus chinensis 'Echiniformis'. This is the tiniest of all junipers, forming a congested globose bush of very small leaves, eventually to 30cm (1ft) or more in height, but very slow growing. Known in cultivation since 1850 it has puzzled gardeners and botanists who previously classified it under *J.communis* and *J.oxycedrus*.

Picea glauca 'Alberta Globe'

Juniperus communis
'Compressa'. First described in 1855, this is the best known miniature conifer of all. It forms tight but slender columns to 45cm (1½ft), sometimes much more, but takes many years to do so.

Picea abies
'Pygmaea'. Known since about 1800, this is one of the oldest miniature conifers. It develops into a broadly domed or shortly pyramidal bush with irregular branches and very short leaves. Under good average conditions it gains about 1.5cm (⅗in) in height per year.

Picea glauca
'Alberta Globe'. This is an even smaller mutation from the popular, slow growing 'Albertiana Conica', with a potential of half the growth rate and size – that is, to only 90cm (3ft) base and 2m (6ft) high.

Pinus leucodermis
'Schmidtii' ('Pygmy', 'Pygmaea'). Found by the late Dr Schmidt in the mountains of Bosnia, this is a real connoisseur's item. It forms a firm dome of dark green, glossy needles, eventually to 25cm (10in) or more high and wide, but must have sharply drained soil to succeed.

Pinus leucodermis 'Schmidtii'

SLOW GROWING

Chamaecyparis pisifera
'Filifera Aurea'. Known since about 1889, this cultivar has some of the pendent branchlets greatly elongated, like small branched whips. In time it can become a broadly conical shrub to 3m (10ft) but takes many years to do so. Grown in a sunny site it can be one of the most vivid golden yellow conifers.

Chamaecyparis lawsoniana
'Gimbornii'. This is one of the smaller, slow growing cultivars, attaining a height of 60cm (2ft) or more. Broadly ovoid in outline it has densely borne sprays of blue-green foliage. It first grew on the Von Gimborn Estate, Doorn, Holland about 1937.

Cryptomeria japonica
'Elegans Compacta'. Less well known than it deserves to be, this is a smaller, neater mutation from the popular 'Elegans'. It has plumy juvenile foliage, green in summer, purple in winter and forms a cloud-like bush, eventually 2m (6ft) tall.

Pinus leucodermis
'Satellit'. The ultimate height of this extremely narrow, erect little pine is unknown, as it is a recent introduction from Holland. However, it seems certain to exceed 150cm (5ft). The leaves are glossy, dark green and curve towards stem.

Tsuga canadensis
'Jeddeloh'. This is a most appealing little bush, eventually spreading to 60cm (2ft) or more, but not quite so tall. It has down-swept sprays of light green foliage that contrast well with darker leaved plants.

Thuja orientalis
'Elegantissima'. This is a columnar bush eventually to 3m (10ft), though fairly slow-growing. It makes a fine accent plant with its yellow, bronze-gold tinted foliage.

Tsuga canadensis 'Jeddeloh'

Thuja orientalis 'Elegantissima'

Juniperus conferta

GROUND COVER

Juniperus conferta.
Introduced in 1915, the Japanese shore juniper is perhaps the finest prostrate species for covering banks and open sunny areas on drier soils. It is generally bright green, but grey and blue phases occur in the wild; 'Blue Pacific' is the best bluish form.

Juniperus sabina
'Blue Danube'. This vigorous cultivar has a tabular habit with a spread of 2.1m (7ft) or more and a height to 90cm (3ft). Despite the name, the foliage is more grey than blue.

Juniperus communis
'Depressa Aurea'. Known since about 1887, this attractive semi-tabular juniper spreads to 1.5m (5ft) or more, with a height of 30-45cm (1-1½ft). The young shoots are bright yellow, ageing to grey-green with bronze tints in winter.

Juniperus communis depressa 'Aurea'

Juniperus sabina 'Blue Danube'

Microbiota decussata.
Discovered in E.Siberia around 1920, this conifer is much like a prostrate thuja with frond-like sprays of scale leaves that turn bronze in winter. It can spread to 2 or possibly 3m (6-10ft) in time.

*Picea abies
'Inversa'. Sometimes this cultivar is trained to a stake to form a small weeping tree. Left to its own devices it covers the ground surprisingly densely and makes ground cover of distinction. It looks particularly effective on a bank.

Picea pungens
'Procumbens'. Also listed wrongly as 'Prostrata', this cultivar has the same appeal as *Picea abies* 'Inversa' but the blue foliage creates a vivid ground haze. Unfortunately, it is prone to produce erect reversion shoots and these must be removed as soon as possible.

SMALLER SPECIMENS

Chamaecyparis lawsoniana
'Fletcheri'. This popular grey-green, juvenile leaved form of Lawson cypress came into the nursery trade in 1911. The best specimens dating from around that time have just topped 13m (42ft), so this cultivar is neither particularly fast nor large. It forms a compact column of great charm and though commonly planted is still worth while.

Juniperus X media
'Pfitzerana'. Like the previously described conifer, this one is much planted but still well worthy of a place in the garden. Where something sizeable but not tall is needed; for example, at one side of a lawn or to end a vista, this juniper is ideal. In time it will top 2.4m (8ft), with a much greater spread.

Juniperus chinensis
'Keteleeri'. In the past identified as a cultivar of *J.virginiana*, this decorative juniper has a conical or columnar habit with dense sprays of rich green scale leaves and usually a profusion of light green fruits.

Chamaecyparis lawsoniana 'Fletcheri'

SIXTY OF THE BEST

Picea abies
'Pumila'. Of charmingly irregular habit, this is suitable for an accent position or rock garden. Can attain 60cm (2ft) or more, is slow growing.

*Thuja occidentalis
'Woodwardii'. Forming a rounded to oval compact bush, this arbor-vitae looks splendid at the end of a modest vista. Attains 90cm (3ft) or more.

Pinus sylvestris
'Beauvronensis'. First described in 1891, this famous mutant of the Scots pine grows to 75cm (2½ft) tall with a greater spread. The grey-green foliage is densely borne and particularly appealing when young and pale in early summer.

Juniperus chinensis 'Keteleeri'

Picea abies 'Pumila'

Pinus sylvestris 'Beauvronensis'

SIXTY OF THE BEST

LARGER SPECIMENS

Chamaecyparis lawsoniana 'Erecta' ('Erecta Viridis'). This rich green, narrowly conical to columnar form of Lawson cypress is a familiar sight in parks and larger gardens. It is particularly effective while young, up to say, 3m (10ft) or so, after which it is best replaced as it often gets untidy or damaged by snow. It is easily grown from cuttings and grows quite fast.

Chamaecyparis nootkatensis. The Nootka cypress comes from north western N.America where it is also known as yellow cypress. It is similar in shape to Lawson cypress but all the upper branchlets are elegantly pendulous. It makes a very fine tree for the larger lawn.

Cupressus macrocarpa 'Donard Gold'. This deep golden-yellow form of Monterey cypress only came on to the market in 1946, so its ultimate height is unknown. It is somewhat slower growing and narrower in habit than the parent species. 'Goldcrest' is also deep yellow but has soft, juvenile foliage.

*Metasequoia glyptostroboides The dawn redwood from China makes a fine lawn tree providing the soil does not dry out, and is excellent for wet places. It is narrowly pyramidal when young, becoming columnar and broadening with age. It can grow 45cm (1½ft) per annum when happily situated. The larch-green leaves are deciduous and take on yellow and russet tints in autumn.

Chamaecyparis nootkatensis

Cupressus macrocarpa 'Donard Gold'

SIXTY OF THE BEST

Picea brewerana.
Brewer's spruce from the Siskiyou Mountains of west U.S.A. is the most beautiful member of its genus. Rather like a Norway spruce in shape, all the side branches hang vertically downwards like shimmering curtains. It is fairly slow growing, especially when young.

Picea purpurea.
Sometimes listed as *P.likiangensis purpurea*, this broadly pyramidal spruce is most distinctive with its upswept branchlet tips. The cones are violet-purple when young. It attains 10-18m (35-50ft) in time.

Metasequoia glyptostroboides

Picea brewerana

Picea purpurea

GREY-BLUE

Chamaecyparis pisifera
'Boulevard'. Much planted in the 50 years it has been known, this juvenile form of the sawara cypress is deservedly popular. It forms a compact, slightly irregular pyramid of steely, blue-grey foliage which seems to glow in evening and morning light. In time it can exceed 2m (6ft).

Juniperus scopulorum
'Table Top Blue'. This selected form of the Rocky Mountain juniper has silvery-blue foliage which takes on a matt-finish in winter. It needs full sun for the best colour. A good ground coverer it rises 75cm (2½ft) or more and can exceed 120m (4ft) in spread.

Juniperus squamata
'Chinese Silver'. In time, this cultivar can rise to 150cm (5ft) with an equal spread. The branches grow up at an angle of 45°, with the tips arching in an elegant fashion. The foliage is of a distinctive silver-blue green.

Picea pungens glauca.
The blue, or Colorado spruce of U.S.A. varies greatly in the wild, from green to blue-white. *P.p.glauca* covers all the bluish-green leaved sorts. From it have arisen the more intensely coloured and generally smaller growing 'Hoopsii', 'Koster' and 'Moerheimii'. 'Globosa' is dwarf and slow growing.

Pinus pumila glauca.
This is the blue-grey leaved compact form of the dwarf Siberian pine. In time it reaches about 45cm (1½ft) in height with a spread of twice this.

Juniperus squamata 'Chinese Silver'

Juniperus scopulorum 'Table Top Blue'

WHITE-CREAM

Chamaecyparis lawsoniana 'Pygmaea Argentea'. Formerly called 'Backhouse Silver', this neat little 30cm (1ft) tall bush has blue-green foliage sprays prominently tipped creamy-white. A suitable candidate for the rock garden.

Chamaecyparis lawsoniana 'Pygmaea Argentea'

Chamaecyparis lawsoniana 'Silver Queen'. Known since about 1883 this tall cultivar has foliage sprays which start creamy-white and gradually age grey-green. The smaller, more broadly pyramidal 'Elegantissima' is brighter and better for the smaller garden.

X *Cupressocyparis leylandii* 'Silver Dust'. Although known for some time, this variegated Leyland cypress is not yet readily available commercially, but doubtless will be in time. In shape and vigour it resembles other selections of this hybrid conifer, but is distinguished by a scattering of white shoot tips.

Cryptomeria japonica 'Sekkan Sugi'. This slow growing cultivar of the Japanese cedar is one of the brightest of conifers in the white/cream range. In summer the leaves are overall creamy-white but as the winter approaches, they take

Chamaecyparis pisifera 'Boulevard'

on bronze tints. It eventually reaches 180cm (6ft) or more.

Juniperus X *media* 'Sulphur Spray'. In growth habit this is similar to 'Pfitzerana', but smaller and less vigorous. Although brighter in the summer it has a creamy-white glow the whole year.

*Thuja occidentalis 'Lutescens'. This cultivar of the eastern arbor-vitae bridges the gap between the white/cream and the yellow/gold categories. The flattened sprays of foliage are whitish-yellow in summer, cream in winter. Forms a conical bush to 150cm (5ft) or more.

YELLOW-GOLD

*Chamaecyparis obtusa 'Nana Lutea'. Small, somewhat rounded sprays of bright golden-yellow foliage make up this delightfully irregular little bush. It eventually reaches 60cm (2ft).

Cupressus macrocarpa 'Horizontalis Aurea'. The plant grown under this name is only relatively "horizontal", being more of an irregularly flat-topped bush to 2.4m (8ft) tall and of greater spread. Its sunny foliage makes it a good accent plant either for the end of a modest vista or by the lawn.

Chamaecyparis obtusa 'Nana Lutea'

Cupressus macrocarpa 'Horizontalis Aurea'

Cedrus deodara 'Golden Horizon'

SIXTY OF THE BEST

Cedrus deodara
'Golden Horizon'. This is a charming, slow growing, almost semi-prostrate form of the deodar, with yellow foliage. It can attain 75cm (2½ft) or more in height and will certainly exceed 120cm (4ft) in time. The cascading growth habit is ideal for banks and dry walls.

Juniperus chinensis
'Kuriwao Gold'. Of New Zealand origin this juniper is probably one of the *chinensis* hybrid (X *media*) group. It has a growth habit akin to that of 'Pfitzerana' but more slender and upright. The densely-borne foliage is golden-green throughout the year.

Taxus baccata 'Fastigiata Aureomarginata'

*Taxus baccata
'Fastigiata Aureomarginata'. This is the golden Irish yew. Broadly columnar to 6m (20ft) tall, it is essentially a specimen tree for the larger garden.

*Thuja plicata
'Rogersii'. First marketed about 55 years ago, this has proved to be a most reliable small gold conifer for the rock garden. The winter bronze suffusion is particularly eye-catching. It forms a slightly irregular, globular to ovoid bush, eventually about 45cm (1½ft) tall.

Juniperus chinensis 'Kuriwao Gold'

Thuja plicata 'Rogersii'

Chamaecyparis lawsoniana 'Mason's Orange'

Cupressocyparis leylandii 'Castlewellan'

X *Cupressocyparis leylandii* 'Leighton Green'

HEDGES/WINDBREAKS

Chamaecyparis lawsoniana. Lawson cypress can be used for hedges and windbreaks. For the latter purpose, one of the strong growing sorts such as 'Glauca' and 'Triomf van Boskoop' (both blue-grey tinted), 'Stewartii' (yellow) and 'Green Pillar' (rich green) should be chosen. Seedlings are just as useful. Almost any of the somewhat smaller, more compact cultivars will make a hedge, but the selection 'Green Hedger' in particular makes a very good background for flower borders or any other garden feature.

X *Cupressocyparis leylandii.* Leyland cypress hardly needs mentioning as it is now the most widely planted conifer in the British

Isles. It can be used effectively as a windbreak, though in very windy sites specimens over 10m (30ft) are liable to break off about halfway. Although it stands clipping well, as a hedge it is best not kept too small.

Cupressus macrocarpa.
Monterey cypress is excellent as a windbreak near the sea. It is not totally hardy and in severe winters can be damaged.

Pinus sylvestris.
Scots pine stands exposed sites well and makes a good cheap windbreak if bought as two or three year old seedlings. The grey-green foliage makes a pleasing background. The same comments go for the Austrian pines *P.nigra*, and the Corsican pines *P.n.maritima*. They are bigger growing and dark green but stand the windiest sites and poorest soils.

**Taxus baccata.*
The common yew makes a first rate hedge, as does its cultivar 'Fastigiata', the Irish yew. The hybrid between Japanese and common yews, *T.X media*, also provides some good hedgers. Best known is 'Hatfieldii', a broadly columnar bush, faster growing than common yew but just as dense, it is male. 'Hicksii' and 'Sargentii' are similar but female. All will make good hedges, 2-3m (6-10ft) in height.

Taxus baccata

INDEX AND ACKNOWLEDGEMENTS

accent trees, 12-13, 38-41
adelgids, 30, 31
alpine beds, 13
animal pests, 31
aphids, 30
arbor-vitae, 20-1

bark, protection, 31
boot-lace fungus, 31

caterpillars, 31
cedars, 16-17
compost
  for cuttings, 26
  garden, 28
  for seeds, 27
conifer, definition, 6
conifer spinning mites, 30
containers, 13
cultivation, 28-9
  maintenance, 29
  planting, 28-9
  pruning, 10, 29
  site, 28
cuttings, 26-7
cypresses, 16-17
  false, 18-20
  Leyland, 18-20

deciduous conifers, 16
digging, 28
diseases, 30-1
drainage, 28
dwarf conifers, 8, 13, 34-5

fertiliser, 28
firs, 14-15

flowers, 6
foliage, 6
  juvenile, 8
  pests and diseases, 30-1
frost, 28
fungicides, 30-1

galls, 31
grafting, 26
green spruce aphid, 30
greenfly, 30
grey-blue trees, 42
ground cover, 11-12, 37-8
hedges, 10-11
  trees for, 46-7
  trimming, 29
hemlock spruces, 15
herbicides, 28
hiba, 21
honey fungus, 31
hormone rooting powder, 26

insecticides, 30-1

junipers, 22-3
juvenile foliage, 9

larches, 16-17
lawns, planting in, 29
leafmould, 29
leaves, 6, 8
  juvenile, 9
  pests and diseases, 30-1
Leyland cypresses, 18-20

lime-free soil, 28

maidenhair, 21
maintenance, 29
manure, 28
mice, 31
miniatures, *see* dwarf conifers
mites, conifer spinning, 30
moth larvae, 31
mulching, 29
mutants, 8

patios, 13
peat, 28, 29
pests, 30-1
phytophthora root death, 31
pines, 14-15
planting, 28-9
propagation, 26-7
  cuttings, 26-7
  grafting, 26
  seed, 26, 27
pruning, 10, 29

rabbits, 31
raised beds, 13, 28
reversion, 8, 26
rock garden, 13
rooting powder, 26

sawflies, 31
screens, 9-10, 46-7
seed, 27
sink gardens, 13
site
  drainage, 28
  soil, 28
siting conifers, 28

slow growing conifers, 8, 36
soil, 28
subsoil, 28
specimen trees, 12-13, 38-41
sports, 8
spruce gall adelgids, 31
spruces, 14-15
squirrels, 31
staking, 29
subsoil, 28
supports, 29
terraces, 13
top soil, 28
training, 29
tubs, 13

voles, 31

watering, 29
waterlogging, 28, 31
weeds
  ground cover, 11-12
  perennial, 28
white-cream trees, 43-4
windbreaks, 9-10, 47-8

yellow gold trees, 44-5
yews, 10, 24-5

Picture credits

Harry Smith Horticultural Photographic Collection: 4/5
Michael Warren: 1
All other pictures: Gillian Beckett

Artwork by

Richard Prideaux and Steve Sandilands